MY BOOK TREE

Blossom Smith

For all the readers
of all of the books
in all of the places

Look at all the rows of
Books inside this tree.
This quaint little place
Is made only for me!

I'm happy to be
Sitting here all alone

I made this sign that says,
"No Bothering Zone!"

What is that extra
Loud buzzing I do hear?

I know it is not
Far away, it's quite near

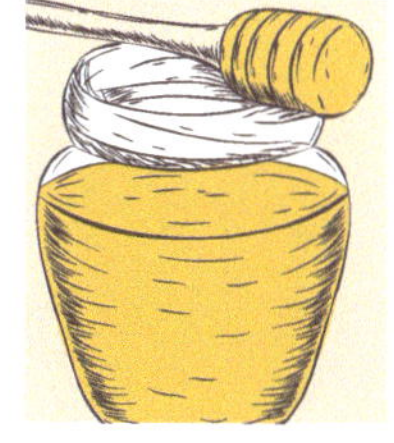

A Bumble Bee!
Bzzz Bzzz

What are you doing
Flying next to my tree?

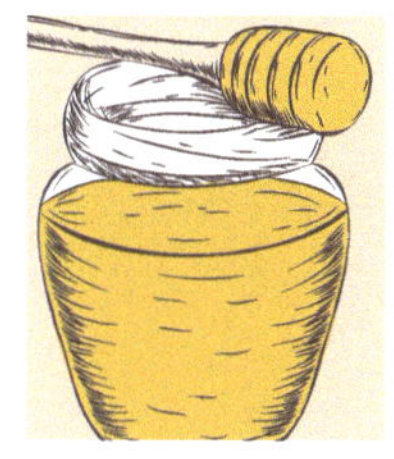

Wait, do you actually
Want to sit with me?

Well, you must agree
To be extra quiet.

This book may be good.
I hope I will like it.

Ouch, now there are
Nuts falling on top of us.

Someone inside this
Tree is making a fuss!

No Bothering Zone
This means you!

It's a Squirrel!
Squeak Squeak

Listen squirrel, I'm begging
You to be quiet.

I cannot read with
This ongoing riot.

I'm determined to start
This lovely story.

I am hoping that
This book won't be boring.

Books about animals

Friendship books
Books about libraries

OK, it seems that now
Everything is fine.

And I'd really like to
Turn the page this time.

There are wonderful
Creatures inside this tree

But my goodness, I just want
To sit and read!

I am so cozy inside
These walls of wood.

Now all of you
Remain Silent, understood?

Oh boy. Now I think
I hear somebody's throat.

The noises come out
Like a very deep croak.

It's a Tree Frog!
Ribbit Ribbit

I'll let you stay if you
Listen and sit still.

I promise it really does
Not take much skill.

Ribbit! Ribbit!
Quack! Quack!
Buzz! Buzz!
Hoo! Hoo!

Thump! Thump!
Wiggle! Wiggle!
Hiss! Hiss!
Moo! Moo!

Hoo Hoo
Bzzz
Ribbit
Ribbit
wiggle wiggle
Ruff
Ruff
Bzzz
Hiss
Hiss
Thump
Thump
Quack
Quack
Moo
Moo

You know what? I do not
Want to YELL and RANT!
But what will come next
Grizzly bears and fire ants?!?!

It really is not a crime to sit and read

BY MYSELF with

MY BOOKS in

MY BOOK TREE!

Oh, what now? I hear a
Little growling sound.

I guess I'll get up and
Search until it's found.

I know I hear it from
Deep inside this place.

Oh wait, I can even
See a tiny face!

A Family of
Possums!

GROWL!
GROWL!

Oh dear Possum,
I've interrupted their sleep.

I'm dreadfully sorry.
That was rude of me.

I'll be very quiet,
Of this I do pledge.

Now close their little eyes
And go back to bed.

Quiet
Who's this story about?
Quiet
Quiet
Shhh
Once upon a time...
Me too!
I thought this was my birthday party.
Zzzz
Zzzz
Shhh
Shhh
Shhh
Shhh
Zzzz
Move over, please.

Oh!

What is that snazzy noise
Coming from outside?

This time, I happily
Put my book aside.

It's a Bird!
Tweet Tweet

So...

I think I've been
Exceptionally crabby,
And her lovely song
Makes me oh so happy.

Go ahead little bird and
Please sing out strong!
I think I've been inside
This tree way too long.

I talk with squirrel, frog, bird,
Bee and the possums.
We decide to do
Something very awesome.

It's a great plan
Because we just decided
To share the book tree.
I'm very excited!

Welcome to the
Free Library Lending Tree!

You can borrow any
Book that you might see.
Just try to put another
Inside the tree.

Dear reader, it's not just
A book tree for me.
It now belongs to
Our great community!

BEE AMAZING
LAW

www.ingramcontent.com/pod-product-compliance
Lightning Source LLC
Chambersburg PA
CBHW041630110726
48005CB00002B/557